Alice

The Life Story of a Yorkshire Girl

Alice

The Life Story of a Yorkshire Girl

by

Alicia Osbourne

The Pentland Press
Edinburgh – Cambridge – Durham – USA

First published in 1995 by
The Pentland Press Ltd
1 Hutton Close
South Church
Bishop Auckland
Durham

British Library
Cataloguing-in-Publication Data
A catalogue record for this book
is available from the British Library.

ISBN 1-85821-250-2

Every word of this story is true,

with the exception of names, which are purely fictitious.

Typeset by Carnegie Publishing, 18 Maynard St., Preston
Printed and bound by Antony Rowe Ltd., Chippenham

To
my son and
two daughters

My Earliest Memories

Rarely did the postman knock on our humble cottage door. But this day, the 28th August 1919, was my fifth birthday.

He had called with a parcel for me. I was so excited. Never before had I had anything through the post.

Mother pulled the string off it and took out a letter which was for her. She let me take out the contents which were a white lace-trimmed pinafore and a rag Charlie Chaplin doll.

I couldn't wait to get the pinafore on, but Mum said it was for Sundays. We wore coloured ones for weekdays. I loved the little doll too, as I didn't have many toys.

When I think about it, I don't suppose there were many toys or luxury items in the shops at that time. It was too soon after the end of the First World War.

My maternal Grandma had sent me the parcel. She would never know how much pleasure she had given me.

The letter seemed to bear bad news. When Dad came home at tea-time he and Mum were discussing it. Dad was furious — he banged his fist on the table and swore. I heard him say: 'Some of them down there could have taken her in and looked after her. Poor old soul. Fancy sending her to the workhouse.'

I asked: 'What is a workhouse?' But I was told to go outside and play with Jamie, my three-year-old brother, and my sister Annie who was nearly two.

The next morning I asked Mum about the workhouse. She said it was an awful place where only the very poor people had to go.

She said Dad's old Grandma had been sent there because she hadn't enough money to pay the rent or buy food with. Plus she was getting too old to look after herself. But Dad thought she had plenty of relatives living near who could have helped her.

The workhouse, I was told, was a place where people had to stop once they got there, unless some other place could be found for them. I felt very sorry for the poor old lady. No wonder Dad was so angry. Especially as she had taken him in and given him a home when his mother had died. He was only nine years old at the time. He must have felt sorry now that he couldn't help her in her time of trouble, but she lived in Cambridgeshire and we were in Yorkshire. Plus, there were five of us in our small cottage and, I'm told, we were very poor ourselves. Wages were low for a farm worker then, which Dad was. If I remember right he only got £1 10s. per week, but we did have a rent and rate-free cottage.

2

School Days

At five years old I should have started school but, as I didn't have very good health, and we were three miles from the nearest school, I was exempt for a year. So it was September of the following year when I started.

I dreaded the thought of going to school. I was so nervous and shy of strangers. Up to then I had not had the chance to mix with people. Also my parents had not helped me with the alphabet or numbers.

I was certainly a raw recruit when I started school.

I shall forever remember that first morning, walking into the classroom. The odd smells and the children all scrambling into their seats. I did not know where to sit, and felt so lost — as I'm sure all children do on their first day at school.

I was seated next to a little girl called Greta. Hers is the only name I remember in that school, and I can still picture her. The poor girl had a hump-back and was as nervous as I was.

We were given a slate and a chalk to write with and copied what the teacher wrote on the blackboard.

Two older girls who lived near us took me to school. It was a long way for us to walk, especially in the winter time.

We had a lot of time off after Christmas when the snow came and the roads would be blocked with drifts, making them impassable for up to a week at a time.

Altogether, I only got just over a year in at that particular school.

One Saturday, towards the end of July, when Dad came home from work, he and Mum had an argument. Apparently he had got the 'sack' and we had to be out of the house in a fortnight.

I was too young to understand what the reason was for him being dismissed — but I do know it caused us much distress.

3

The Journey Down South

The next thing I remember was being on a train going south to Grandma's. What happened to our home I never knew, not that we had a great deal of furniture.

All we had *now* was one box of clothes and small oddments.

That train journey has stayed very clear in my mind. I sat near the window and gazed at the telegraph wires as they seemed to go up and down. I could not understand why they seemed to do that.

Every so often a cloud of smoke from the engine would block my view. All the time I was wondering what our Grandparents were like and what we were going to do there.

4

My Grandparents

Grandpa met us at the station with a horse and trap. He was a tall, gentle type of man. I liked him. I remember him asking Mum how old I was and she said I was seven. I thought it wicked of her to tell a lie as I was not seven years old for another three weeks. It's funny how such little things stick in one's mind for so long.

I didn't like getting into that trap. I had never been in one before. There was not room for Dad or the box. Grandpa had to go back for them. Luckily they lived only about a mile from the station.

I can still picture my Grandparents' little thatched cottage with its pretty garden at the front and rambling roses climbing up the wall.

Auntie Annie, Mum's youngest sister, was waiting for us at the garden gate. She led us up the path and into the house, where Grandma was preparing a meal. I thought how cosy it was, with nice lino on the floor, pretty curtains at the window and lots of pictures and photographs on the walls. There was a large 'clipped' rug in front of the fireplace and lots of ornaments on the mantleshelf and the sideboard.

I wished we could stay there for good, but I had been told that we were only there until Dad could find another house and work.

After the greetings were over Grandpa walked into the kitchen and came out with a glass of milk. Looking at me he said: 'Here you are, Duckie, drink this. It's goats' milk, it will do you good.'

I didn't like milk at all. I had never heard of goats' milk, but he insisted I drink it. So, just to please him, I drank a little then handed it to Jamie.

Grandma then suggested we go and see the goats, so Grandpa took us into the kitchen, through the back door into the garden, and up the long path into a paddock where he kept three goats. They looked at us as though they objected to our presence there. I was very pleased to get back into the garden.

Grandpa said he would have to dig some potatoes up for tomorrow's dinner and I could help him pick them up. We also picked peas and shelled them. He had a big vegetable garden.

Soon after tea we were packed off to bed, we always had to go early. Grandma was a very strict person, well, she had brought up a family of ten. So I suppose children had to be seen and not heard, and she wasn't granting us any favours.

Looking back, I'm sure she felt she hadn't elbow room in that small cottage with an extra five of us in it.

If my memory serves me right, we were only there about ten days. Each morning there seemed to be a row.

Jamie used to cry such a lot at night and keep them all awake. Then, to crown it all, he wet the bed. That really did it. She said we would have to leave.

I thought she was a nasty old thing, but we could not stop there indefinitely. They wouldn't have much money either after bringing all that family up.

At that time, of course, they were all grown up and working away in different places. Some of them were married.

There was just Annie at home. She had recently left school and was looking for a job. We didn't see much of her as she went to live with an older, married sister while we were there, to make sleeping room for us.

4

But *now* we had outstayed our welcome. I couldn't help but wonder where we should go next.

5

On The Move Again

This time it was no train journey. We had to walk.

We left our Grandparents soon after dinner at noon. Someone had given Mum an old pram so little Annie was sat under the hood and Jamie sat across the bottom. I, of course, had to walk.

On and on we went. My poor legs ached. I asked if we were going to another house and was told yes. I said I hoped it would be like Grandma's, but I got no answer to that.

At last we could see the town ahead of us. I was so pleased. I kept wondering what our house would be like. But, more to the point, what would there be for tea. With all that walking I was feeling very hungry.

Just then Jamie wanted to 'pee', so we stopped at the next gateway. Dad took him behind the hedge. Then he shouted to Mum to bring the pram through into the field.

They suggested we all sit down and have a rest for a while — we were certainly ready for it. I would rather have kept going till we got to our house. We drank the water which we had brought in bottles, and sat there so long it was beginning to get dusk. I kept asking when we were going but was told to keep quiet. Dad was going to fetch us some fish and chips. I simply could not understand why we didn't all go and have the fish in our house instead of sitting there when it was getting cold and dark.

In retrospect, I suppose they had not the heart to tell me the truth.

By the time Dad arrived back with the fish and chips they were cold, but we were so hungry it didn't matter much.

Having eaten mine I got up to go but was promptly told to sit down. In fact I was told to lie down and cuddle Jamie to keep us warm. I cried myself to sleep, and hate welled up in my heart for both parents for the plight we were in. I knew I would never forgive them. At that time I still did not know the worst.

I awoke to the sound of a cock crowing across the meadow. It was just breaking daylight. I realised we had slept out all night and was horrified and ashamed. I was barely seven years old but felt it as much as if I was seventeen.

I looked across the meadow and could just see the roofs and chimneys of some cottages and wondered if the people would come and tell us to get out.

At last we set off to town. That is, after we had all been to the toilet 'behind the bushes.' It did not take us long to get to the town. I was feeling a bit happier now, but impatient to see our house. As we walked along the street we came to some very large iron gates with a smaller gate at the side. We all stopped and looked through. Mum and Dad were arguing again.

Just inside the small gate was a hut with a man sat inside. Dad said something to him and he opened the small gate and let us through.

We had to walk down a path and knock on the door of this large building. A middle-aged woman dressed in navy with a silly white hat on her head — at least I thought it was silly — opened the door. She took us to what I imagined was our house, unlocked the door, and told us to sit down. She said she would bring us a drink.

In the room was a large table in the middle with seats all around the walls. I thought it looked different to any house I had seen before.

It was not long before the woman returned with a tray full of mugs of cocoa and a plate of bread and margarine. We were very thankful for it. By the time we had finished, the same woman came back and told Dad he must go with her. He kissed us all goodbye and told Mum not to worry, he would soon have us out again.

The 'penny still had not dropped' with me. I said to Mum: 'Where are we?'

She replied: 'It's the bloody workhouse. That's where your rotten father has landed us.'

I was absolutely stunned and horrified and could not believe it. To think we were in that dreadful place where, as she had said only a few months before, that one never gets out again, unless very lucky.

Mum was crying, broken-hearted, but I could feel no pity for her — only hatred for the way they had dragged us down. I knew then that I should never forget that dreadful time.

It has proved true. All my life it has hung over me like a black cloud. Never once have I ever told anyone — only lived in fear of someone getting to know. I have always downgraded myself as a result of it and never felt that I was as good as anyone else.

But, to get back to my story. We, that is Jamie, Annie and I, were taken away from Mum through the door which we had first knocked on and down a long, flagged corridor in the main part of the building. At the bottom I was told to stand still while she, the nurse, took Jamie and Annie, who were both crying, into the nursery.

When she came back she led me in the opposite direction to a ward full of women. We walked past a few beds and I was given the last one on the left-hand side.

The nurse told me to lay my coat on the locker and she would soon come back. I felt all eyes were on me and was trying hard not to cry. The woman in the bed next to mine asked me my name. I didn't feel like speaking to her so just said: 'Alicia Osbourne.'

She said: 'My word, that's a mouthful. Can I call you Alice?' She told me that was her Mother's name.

I said yes, in answer to her question, after all most people did call me that. Only my Mother and Grandma insisted on Alicia. I had been christened after my maternal Grandma, being her first grandchild.

The woman in the bed said I could call her Emma, and that the one next to her was Lily.

6

More Shocks

The nurse returned carrying a towel over her arm and a saucer in her hand. She led me into a big cold-looking bathroom, the likes of which I had never seen before.

The worst shock was that huge bath. I thought I should drown in it. The only bath I had been in was a small zinc one placed in front of the fire. I had problems getting in this large white porcelain one and the nurse had to help me. Once in it, she poured a jug of water over my head. Then with a tablet of carbolic soap rubbed it into my hair. It pulled my hair and brought tears to my eyes. Then another jug of water being poured over to rinse it.

After washing me all over, she helped me out and dried me. Then I found out what the saucer was for. It had vinegar and a small toothcomb on it. She combed and combed my hair till my head was sore. I was pleased she did not find any 'livestock.'

7

Then, horror of horrors, she put this awful calico nightie on me. It was like an operating gown, fastened down the back. What really upset me was the fact that it had lost the strings off the lower half. I was sure all the women in the ward would see my bare bottom when I walked back to my bed. For a modest child like me that was very upsetting.

The nurse walked to the bed with me and helped me in. I pulled the sheet up over my head and cried as never before — heartbroken over the chain of events.

I could hear Emma saying: 'Don't cry Duckie, you'll be all right here. We'll look after you.' Finally I fell asleep. It was dinner time when I awoke.

I was brought a plate of minced beef, mashed potato and cabbage and had to admit I had enjoyed it, although feeling so utterly miserable. After dinner the doctor came and examined me. I felt very nervous of him, but remembered he was a very nice man. He said I must stay in bed two or three days. I never knew why.

When he had gone, the nurse brought me some comics to look at. I still could not read so it didn't take me long to look at them. Emma started talking to me, asking me a lot of questions. I strongly objected to that as I hated people asking me questions. Yet Lily was the one who alarmed me the most.

She had long ginger-coloured hair and kept staring at me. Her mouth kept opening and shutting, but no sound came out. She was gesturing with her hands. I suppose Emma could see I was alarmed so she told me that Lily was deaf and dumb and I would have to learn her language. I was very doubtful of ever doing that.

Surprisingly, I did learn enough of it to be able to understand at least some of what she said, also she could understand me.

I don't know what I should have done in that place if Emma and Lily had not been so kind to me. After all, the nurses had not time to bother with me.

I was kept in bed for three or four days. Then I was allowed to get up and join the others in the 'day room' as it was called.

I hated the clothes I had to wear and did not understand why I could not wear my own. I never saw them again.

The dress they gave me to wear was dark grey and rough looking. I had to wear long black woollen stockings, which I had a problem keeping up even with elastic garters. My legs were too thin for them. I also had lace-up boots.

One morning, in the day room, I remember well Emma was having a glass of Andrews Liver Salts. I stood there looking at her and wishing I could have some, it looked so good. As though she was reading my thoughts, Emma asked me if I would like some.

I promptly said: 'Yes, please,' but regretted it later when it fizzed up my nose and into my eyes. I got more than I had bargained for. Putting the glass on the table I said: 'By gum, it's fizzy.' They all howled with laughter at my Yorkshire accent. Needless to say, I didn't laugh. The time came when the school holidays were over. It was now September, (I must have had my seventh birthday without even knowing it). I was told I would have to start school and that I could live in the same quarters as the other children. It was in a different part of the building. In fact it was next to the reception room, where we had been taken on our arrival at the workhouse.

If I remember correctly, there were about nine girls there, but I only remember the names of the two older ones. They were Dolly and Hilary and would be about twelve years old. They had to take us younger ones to school.

I felt very nervous about meeting more strangers and did not like the way I got laughed at for my broad Yorkshire accent.

I don't know how it was that I had an accent — my parents did not seem to pick it up at all. We were born in Cambridgeshire, and our grandparents before us. We had moved to Yorkshire, so I was told, about half-way through the Great War.

Dad had been in the army in France, Belgium and Egypt, but had been discharged through ill health, or a wound, I'm not sure which. As there was no work where they lived, they moved to Yorkshire, and were lucky enough to get work and a house on a farm. That house which we had to leave so sharply. So I must have picked up my accent during my short time there.

Children soon pick up accents.

7

My New School

I settled in well at my new school. It was a nice walk there and not such a long walk as my last school.

Perhaps the best part was getting away from that workhouse for a few hours each day.

I had nice teachers who helped me with reading and writing. By Christmas I was getting on fine, could read all the infant books, and was feeling a bit happier.

Christmas was a 'non-event.' No presents or cards. The only thing that was different from any other day was a dinner of turkey and all the trimmings, with plum pudding and custard to follow.

We were taken into the big dining hall, which the inmates had decorated with paper chains that they had made themselves. There was a huge tree in one corner of the room, but not many decorations on it.

After dinner, which we always had at noon, us girls had to go back to our quarters. Dolly and Hilary had put a few chains up in the room. They also put on a little concert of their own, which did not amuse me when it came to my turn to perform.

They put tinsel round my head and a sparkler in my hand. Then I had to stand on a box and sing!! I even remember the song, it was 'O Star of Eve.' I was always too scared to talk, let alone sing.

8

Jamie Starts School

When we started school again after the Christmas holidays, Jamie had to go to school. He had had his fifth birthday in December.

I had not seen him since that awful day when we arrived at the workhouse. He seemed to have altered.

By the time I got him to school and seated at his desk, I wished I had not seen him *then*. He screamed and yelled nearly all day. I was fetched out of my class to try to quieten him, but it was impossible as he did not want to know anything about school. The second day was nearly as bad. He tormented me with his crying. In all his school days he never was much of a scholar.

However, he settled down eventually and made friends with another boy, which was just as well, because in February I was taken ill again and off school for a couple of weeks.

I woke up one morning in the dormitory feeling terrible. Dolly was trying to get me up for school, but I was sick all over the floor. They sent for matron who said I had measles and must go into the isolation ward with two other girls who had it. I spent two weeks there.

9

A Surprise

Just a few days before I was taken ill with the measles the nurse met me as I arrived back from school. She said my mother wanted to see me. She then led me down a long corridor and into a small room on the left hand side.

What a surprise I got. There was Mum laid in bed. She said: 'Hello, Alicia, come round this side of the bed and see what I have got.' There, in bed with her, was this tiny baby with black hair and a red wrinkled face. It was a boy. I was speechless, and could not believe she would get another baby when they did not have money or a home for us three. I said to her: 'Where did it come from?'

She said the doctor brought it in his black bag and I, of course, believed her.

I hadn't the slightest clue where they came from, Mums are not supposed to tell lies. She looked thrilled to bits with him — but I was not. I was taken again the next day to see them. This time Mum asked me if I knew a nice name for him. I told her I did not know any boys' names only one, that was Douglas. He was a little boy who walked home from school with us. He was an 'outsider,' not an inmate of the workhouse. Mum said it was a nice name, so he was called Douglas William. I didn't see Mum or the baby for a long time after that visit. It didn't seem to worry me.

10

Lucy

After recovering from the measles and leaving the isolation ward, I was sent back to the women's ward. This time I was put in the first bed on the left-hand side.

Each morning a nurse took me up the corridor to meet the girls, so they could take me to school. A different nurse used to take Jamie as he was still in the nursery with Annie and the other younger ones.

One afternoon, on arriving back from school, I walked up to my locker to put something in, and there, in my bed, was a young girl called Lucy. She was fourteen years old.

I had to go back to the bed near Emma. She and Lily were pleased to see me. They wanted to know about school and what I had been doing since I left the ward.

Lucy and I became good friends, but sadly she was not there for long. I have often wondered since what she was there for at all and was very sorry when she left.

She did me a good turn before she left. She asked me if I would like to go and spend a weekend with her at her home. It was all arranged with the Matron, and at Easter I was taken to the station and put on the train with strict instructions where to get off. It was only two stations further on. I was very nervous about going on a train by myself, yet at the same time excited about seeing Lucy and her parents.

It turned out they were not her parents, but her grandparents. I don't know why she lived with them. Perhaps she was an orphan.

However, she met me at the station as arranged and we walked up a road to the village. Before going to her house we had to call at the vicarage. We went to the back door and were invited into the kitchen by the maid. She gave us some lemonade and biscuits. Soon the vicar appeared and spoke to us. As we left he said he would see us in church on Sunday morning.

We proceeded to Lucy's house. It was very much like my grandparent's inside, so homely and nice.

In the afternoon we went for a walk and Lucy called for her friend who lived further down the village. She was about the same age as Lucy. They said they would take me into the meadow and pick some flowers. At one side of the meadow was a wood, and it really was a lovely sight. I will never forget it — a carpet of bluebells and snowdrops. At the edge of the wood was a grassy bank covered in primroses. We spent the afternoon picking flowers, I had not felt so happy for a long time.

On the Sunday morning we had to go to church. When the vicar came in he stopped at our pew and spoke to us. He also gave us a silver threepenny piece each. My world! I was over the moon with delight. I had never had that much money before, at least not all at once. I sat there thinking which sweets I would buy. Perhaps a pennyworth of aniseed balls and some dolly mixtures and save the remaining penny.

My thoughts and hopes were dashed, however, when Lucy turned to me as the last hymn was being sung and said: 'Have you got your money ready? The man will be coming soon with the collection plate. Then you must put it on.'

I can't describe my disappointment at that moment — I thought it was a dirty trick of that vicar to give me money then take it back.

He redeemed himself the next day when I had to return 'home.' We had to call at the vicarage again, and the vicar walked with us to the station. On the platform he gave me another threepenny piece, plus a comic, also an apple to eat on the train. All was forgiven. I was able to start planning again how to spend it.

Lucy said I could go again in the summer holiday.

I often wondered what the vicar had to do with my visits there. Perhaps he was a governor of the workhouse.

11

The Cinema

Each Saturday afternoon we were allowed to go to the pictures. I can still see us workhouse kids lined up on one side of the foyer and the 'outsiders,' as we called them, lined up on the other side. They used to stare at us as though we were some lesser beings.

However, all that was forgotten when we were seated inside and the lights were out. The film was usually a Charlie Chaplin or Buster Keaton one. Silent films and black and white of course. It was the highlight of the week and, I can truthfully say, the only time we could laugh and feel happy.

I was able to spend my money at the sweet shop nearby.

12

Settling Down in My New 'Abode'

When we started back to school after the Easter holidays, we were given some new dresses to wear. They were blue check gingham. I was so pleased with mine as it was such a change after the awful grey ones we wore all winter. It's amazing what a new dress can do for a little girl's morale.

By this time I was feeling more settled in my new abode (I could hardly call it home). The weather was much better, which pleased me, as I never could stand the cold.

We were now allowed to play in the meadow at the side of the school. It was covered in buttercups and daisies, and we spent all the play time making daisy chains and picking buttercups to take to the teacher.

There was a large white gate leading into the meadow which we could not resist swinging on when we thought no-one was looking. We regretted it later when, one child after another got ringworms on arms and legs. I got one on the top of my head. It was not discovered until the 'nit nurse' came. She wrote a note for me to take back to the Matron. The result was I had to have the top of my head shaved and, worse still, had to wear an awful grey mop cap. I was so upset, thinking everyone would stare at me.

It was said we got the ringworms off that gate through the cattle having them and rubbing themselves on the gate.

I go to Lucy's Again

The summer passed all too quickly and I wondered when I would be able to go to Lucy's again. Nothing more had been said about her.

However, about half-way through the summer holidays, the nurse came one morning to tell me there was a letter from Lucy's Grandma saying I could go the following weekend. I was so excited at the thought of seeing Lucy again.

My ringworm had cleared up and the nurse said my hair was growing again. I was delighted to be rid of that awful cap.

I was put on the train again — all the same procedures taking place as at Easter.

The only disappointment for me was that all the lovely flowers had died off in the wood. We had to pick brambles off the hedge instead. Lucy had taken a large can to put them in and so did her friend. It was not very easy for me as most of them were out of my reach, and they were very prickly.

We went to church again on the Sunday morning, receiving our threepenny piece for the collection plate. This time I was prepared for what I had to do with it.

On the Monday morning I was put on the train by Lucy and the vicar — again he gave me threepence and comics. Sad to say, that was the very last I ever saw or heard of them. Many times over the years I've thought of Lucy.

Summer Holidays Over

Back to school again. The long holiday was over, but school was not such an awesome place for me now. I could read and write a bit and had made a few friends, which made life a bit easier.

Christmas came round again. Everything was the same again as the previous one. Nothing to get excited about.

I can't remember much about that winter, nor the following spring, except that we were still in the workhouse.

One afternoon, about the end of July, we were told we could take our tea, 'our bread and scrape,' onto the lawn to eat. While we sat there, Mother came looking for me and said Dad had run away during the night. She was expecting him to write and let her know where he was. Hopefully he would have found work and a house for us.

She had a long wait. It was the middle of October before she heard from him. She came and told me that he had got work, and a house, somewhere in Yorkshire. Also that I should have to mind my Ps and Qs when we got there. To this day, I still do not know what those Ps and Qs stand for. I did not understand why she should speak to me thus as I had not done anything wrong.

She was a funny woman.

15

We go back to Yorkshire

The day came towards the end of November when we left the workhouse. I was excited to think we were going to live as a family again, and tried to visualise the house, hoping it would be like Grandma's.

I also felt sad at leaving the girls behind and can still picture them waving us off, and asking me to write to them. I said I would but had my doubts as to my ability to write a letter. Perhaps I ought to have been able to, yet I was still only nine years old and not quite up to most children of that age.

I felt sorry for them having to stay there, and also felt sorry for Emma and Lily — they had been so good to me. Yet, as happened with Lucy, that was the very last I ever saw and heard of them.

I can even remember what I wore that day. Someone had knitted me a blue and fawn horizontal striped jumper, and a hat with a bobble on.

It seemed a long way to Yorkshire on the train. I sat near the window again and watched the telegraph lines go up and down as I had done two years previously. There were no animals to be seen this time, it was too cold for them to be outside.

By the time we reached our destination it was getting dark. The farmer and dad were at the station to meet us with the farmer's car. He drove us the three miles to our cottage on the farm.

What a shock I got. My grand illusions of a nice home were shattered. There was next to no furniture in the place, only a dirty looking old table, which needed a good scrubbing, and two old wooden chairs. Nothing on the brick floor, no curtains at the window, no beds, only a couple of straw mattresses on the living room floor and, worst of all — no food, except for a loaf of bread, some margarine, a pot of jam and a can of milk.

Dad made a fire but there was only sticks to burn, which didn't send out much heat and soon burned away. This was even worse, much worse, than the workhouse. I cried and said I was not going to stay there, I was going to run away.

Earlier that day I had felt sorry for the girls in the workhouse — now I felt they were the lucky ones. I would have given anything to have gone back. The shame and misery I felt at that time has never left me.

Luckily Jamie, Annie, and not forgetting baby Douglas, were all too young to remember those days. As far as I know they were never told. I can't remember any of us ever mentioning the workhouse again once we were out of it.

That winter must have been the worst that any of us have ever experienced. I hated my parents and blamed them for the plight we were in, having no respect for them for the rest of their lives. I know times were very bad for all working class people between the two wars, but everyone else seemed to manage so much better than us.

I suppose, looking back, it was Dad's fault for not sticking to his jobs. I never found out why he didn't, as he was a nice chap really, not seeming to be afraid of work. He spent long hours on the farm, even on Sundays.

Mother wasn't the best of housekeepers, and hopeless at cooking. Of course the poor woman had nothing to make use of and very little money to buy household goods with. The weekends were the best time for us when Dad got his wages. Mum was able to get some meat and at least make a decent Sunday dinner. Yet by Thursday the money had all gone — and so had the food.

I well remember winter afternoons returning from school, cold and hungry, raiding the pantry for any crust I could find. If there was no margarine left, I would break the crust up, put it in a cup and pour boiling water on it. With the addition of salt and pepper I pretended it was soup.

I could tell some tales about that winter which would be hard to believe.

17

We Start Another School

The first Monday after arriving at the farm we had to start school. There were quite a few children from the other cottages on the farm to walk there with. Once again I was getting laughed at, for my 'southern' accent this time. They little knew what I thought of their Yorkshire dialect. One had to be born there to understand it.

One day in class, a little boy made fun of me. The teacher told him I was the one who spoke properly, so then I was dubbed teacher's pet.

It was another very cold winter and we had three miles to walk to school. We soon wore out our shoes, so I often went with holes in the soles.

Christmas came round again and, although I was nine years old, I still liked to believe in Santa Claus. Therefore I expected a bit more in my stocking — which we hung on the foot of the bed — than the few monkey nuts and an orange that *he supposedly* brought.

I could never understand why the better-off children always got nice toys, such as dolls, books and even bicycles — they already had more than us. I did not know whether to blame God or Santa Claus. They were both supposed to be good — though not to us.

During the holidays the snow came down thick and fast. The road leading from the farm up to the main road, was blocked with drifts of snow up to the hedge tops. So we had more time off school, which did not help our education.

It was not much fun stopping at home. We could only afford one bag of coal per week and, when that had gone we had to rely on sticks, which were none too plentiful in winter.

Spring Time

Spring has always been my favourite time of year, and that year was really good for us.

A farmer not far from us was selling up 'lock, stock and barrel', as the saying goes. Everything on the farm and in the house had to go. Dad borrowed a horse and cart and went to the sale. He arrived back with furniture, bedding, pots and pans, old rugs and lino. We were really 'set up' — at last we had a decent home. In fact, we had some nicer furniture than the neighbours.

How Dad paid for it all I never knew, but I had a feeling most of it was given. Probably it wouldn't sell, and they had to get rid of it somehow. By Easter, Dad had planted the garden up with potatoes and vegetables. There was also soft fruit bushes and a couple of apple trees. So by the middle of summer, we had plenty to eat. Things were really looking up for us.

We all used to go into the nearby wood and gather sticks, trying to get a good pile in for winter. Of course we had to have a fire all through the summer, as that was our only means of cooking, or even boiling a kettle. We could let it out when not needed.

The Flower Show

That summer us children were asked to enter in the Wild Flower Section of the show. So, on the Friday night, I set off to find a bunch of flowers from the road side.

Dad insisted on coming with me. I was furious, I wanted to pick them myself. He picked every kind of flower and grasses that there was — I had to use both hands to hold them. He tied them up with a dirty, old piece of string and 'plonked' them into the biggest jam jar he could find. I cried myself to sleep that night because I didn't want to take them.

The next day we walked to the village with the flowers resting in the corner of the pram. I walked into the school with the flowers and placed them with all the others. I wished the floor would open and swallow me up when I saw the other girls with their bunches. Some had half-a-dozen wild roses tied up with pink satin ribbon, while others had a few white dog daisies tied with red ribbon, and so on.

I wondered which of the girls would burst out laughing first at my effort, but I was ignored and felt they pitied me. However, I got the surprise of my life when I went to fetch them away at five o'clock. Lo and behold, mine had the first-prize ticket on!! The judge said I had put the most effort into mine. So I had to thank Dad.

The only other prize I ever won at school was one each year, from ten to thirteen years old, for religion.

Soon after the flower show we broke up for the summer holidays. One day Mum took us to town, which was a real treat for us. We had to walk the three miles into the village and get on the carrier's van. He ran it into town every Thursday, which was market day. There were no buses then — at least not round that area.

Mum gave us a penny each to spend on sweets. She wanted to go to the second-hand shop to rig us all up with clothes. Regardless of whether they fitted us or not, we had to wear them.

We went to the fish and chip shop for dinner — that was a real treat for us. We did enjoy it and wished we could go more often.

By the time we had walked the three miles back home from the village, we were tired out.

There is one incident of that summer that will remain with me for ever.

The farmer had a pit in the corner of one of his fields into which they threw all their rubbish. Often this was stuff that we could make use of — especially when the farmer's wife had been turning her cupboards out. So on this Thursday, when we knew they would be at the market, Jamie and I went to the pit to see what we could find.

The thing that took my eye was a tin, which I thought had some kind of icing sugar in it. I stuck my finger in and scooped up as much as I could and put it in my mouth. Luckily Jamie did not get any of it. I thought I was going to choke to death as it stuck like glue all around my mouth and got fast on my teeth. Try as I might, I could not get it out. I started to cry, which started Jamie crying as well. We hurried home, taking the tin with us. Mum was panic stricken and said she ought to send for the doctor in case it was poisonous, but she could not afford to pay him. It took hours to get the horrible stuff out of my mouth.

What a pity it was I could not read the larger words, as I should then have known not to eat it. Instead of icing sugar it was izing glass and was used for preserving eggs. Of course we did not have any eggs to preserve or I might have known what it was.

I know it was the most vile stuff I have ever tasted, and was lucky not to have been poisoned.

19

Another Surprise

We had been back at school a couple of weeks when, arriving back home one day in the afternoon, there was one of the neighbours in our house — and no sign of Mum. When I asked where she was Betty, the neighbour, said: 'Go upstairs, you'll see her.'

You've guessed it! There she was in bed with another baby boy. I could not believe it — how could she be so stupid when we were so poor.

He was christened George, and grew into a lovely little boy. By the winter I was very interested in him — in spite of my first thoughts — and I used to hurry home from school so I could play with him.

Bad luck dogged us once again when I got whooping cough and, one by one, so did the rest of the family, including little George. We coughed and choked for weeks and none of us ever got a good night's sleep. Mum had to send for the doctor, (whether he ever got paid or not I would not know). He said we must stay in bed, keep warm, and get plenty of nourishing food into us. 'What a laugh!'

Mum had to sit up with Georgie most nights. One morning, after I had been in bed a week or so, I walked downstairs to find Mum crying, broken hearted. Poor little Georgie was dead. We both cried till we had no tears left.

I can still see the undertaker carrying the little white coffin out of the house. Dad was the only one to go to the funeral as Mum could not leave us. That was my first brush with death — but not my last.

More Bad News

That spring brought more bad news, although my parents must have known it was coming.

The farmer retired, so all his employees had to find somewhere else to work and live. All except a couple, who were asked to stop on for the next farmer. No such luck for us.

Dad was out of work for a month or more, with no money coming in and no dole in those days, only what was called Parish Pay. That was not actually money, it was a voucher which we took to the village shop and could only have the bare necessities.

We had more meal times than meals during those few weeks.

Dad Gets Another Job

I did not mind the move as it was nearly twenty miles further away, so I thought no-one there would know about us being in the workhouse. Almost every day of my life I have worried about people finding out. It was silly of me. After all, we should have been, and perhaps were, pitied not condemned.

Again the school was three miles away — another long walk for us. This was especially so for little Annie, who had just started at the last school. She was not very strong and I used to think how lucky the village children were, to be so near the school. They didn't have the walking we had, often in bad weather, and we had to be in school on time or were in trouble. The farm where Dad was now working was half-way to the village. The farmer and his wife had just one daughter, called Frances, who was the same age as me. We used to walk to and from school together, and became firm friends. To this day we still are. We have shared all our troubles and joys together, and I cannot remember us ever having an argument.

We picked the wild flowers that grew by the road side, knowing them all by name, and looked for birds' nests in the spring.

In autumn it was the brambles which grew on the hedges we picked, and ate. Sometimes we would raid the nearest turnip field and get a young turnip, 'bash' the root end of it on the gate, and eat it on the way home. They were delicious, especially when one is hungry as I usually was. The house we had was a bit bigger than the last one. Again it had a good big garden with soft fruit bushes and apple trees. Once Dad had planted it up and the stuff began to grow, we were all right for food. There was a very big wood close to our house, so we always had a good supply of sticks. We spent hours in the summer time playing in that wood. Things were beginning to look up a bit for us.

I remember my Grandma came to stay with us the second summer that we were there. She brought Annie and I a new dress each. It was a treat to have something new at last. She had made them herself, and they certainly looked home-made. They fitted where they touched.

Sad to say I got to the wrong side of her, not over the dresses though, it was something quite different.

We were packed off to school the first morning she was there, with our jam sandwiches wrapped up in newspaper and having had some watery porridge for breakfast. We had not gone far when I remembered that I had not got my homework, so I had to go back for it. As I approached the front door I could smell a mouth-watering aroma of bacon and eggs. I was furious that we could not have had the same, after all we did have a long walk.

To make a long story short, I told them both what I thought of them — but not until I got to the door on my way out. I was a bit nervous of going home after school, as I thought I might get punished for my cheek, but I got off rather lightly.

All the same, Grandma never forgave me. I learned a few years later that she had told her relations back home that I was a cheeky kid, and nothing near as nice as Annie. She forgot that Annie had not smelled that bacon and eggs frying.

Apparently Grandma had come for a reason. It was while she was with us that another baby boy arrived, (a few more, I thought, and we shall have a football team). She had come to look after Mum and the house. Mothers always seemed to stop in bed for a fortnight in those days.

The new baby was christened Lawrence. At nearly two years old, just when he was at his most appealing, the poor little lad was struck down with polio. He was very ill for a week and the doctor said we must prepare ourselves for the worst. We were all devastated, the thought of another death in the family was much too much.

Luckily he pulled through, although not altogether lucky for him, as he was left with one leg paralysed. He had a few stays in hospital but nothing seemed to help.

He wore a caliper on his leg for the rest of his life. In my opinion he was the nicest one of the family, always smiling and cheerful, in spite of his affliction.

22

My First Lesson in Sex

I still was not sure where these babies came from, except what I had learned at the last school from a girl two years older than me, called Margery Gibbon.

One morning at playtime, she approached my friend Laura and I to tell us they had a new baby girl at their house. I asked her if Dr. Mathews had brought it. She looked at me scornfully and said: 'No, ya stupid. Doctors don't bring 'em, they grow in your mother's belly.' With that she ran off to her friend.

Laura and I stood there 'gob-smacked' as they say in Yorkshire. I didn't believe a word of it and thought she was pulling our legs. It sounded too horrible to believe. Laura said: 'How would they get it out without cutting her belly open?' The more we thought about it the worse it got. There was another question — How did it get in there? Curiosity got the better of Laura and I. We decided that the first time we got the chance we were going to ask her.

It was a few days before she came up to us and told us their new baby was going to be called Christine. Laura said to her: 'How can a baby get into anybody's belly?'

Margery replied: 'You two are dumb. Don't ya know nowt?' She then proceeded to tell us her version of sex and birth. Her language and version of it was quite unprintable. We could not have had a worse person to give us our first lesson.

It would not have been any use me asking my Mother about it — she would just have told me to run out and play. Such subjects were not mentioned in our house.

23

Helen

The second summer that I was at the school was a good one, as regards the weather. Come to think of it, most summers were good, and the winters bad.

Frances and I had got friendly with a girl called Helen, who used to walk the same way as us. She sometimes invited me to her house in the holidays. I liked her mother — she was very kind to me — but I liked her cooking even better! She made some lovely dinners and the best cakes and pastries I had ever tasted. I did so wish my Mum could have cooked like that. Of course, as I have said before, my Mum didn't have the ingredients or the tools to work with which they had in a big farmhouse.

Helen's Dad was not actually the farmer, he was the foreman. All the single men who worked on the farm used to have bed and board in the foreman's house. In Yorkshire it was called the *hind* house. I never knew why it was so called.

So, of course, Helen's Mum was always a busy woman — always seemed to be cooking or washing up.

They did not stay long at the farm, moving some distance away. I missed them at first, then I caught up with them again some months later as I will tell.

24

My Last Year at School

I was thirteen years old by now, and looking forward to leaving school. Never being much of a scholar, I did not enjoy school. However, my

25

schooldays were brought to an abrupt end through illness. There was an epidemic of scarlet fever going around. About ten children out of our school got it — I was one of the last.

I spent six long weeks in the isolation hospital, and hated it at first. Yet by the end of my stay, I did not want to go home.

My schooldays ended because they broke up for the summer holidays the same week that I went home. I had my fourteenth birthday during the holiday.

Then I had to start looking for work. The doctor told Mum I had to get built-up before I started work. He realised that I was not 'fitted' for anything but domestic work — that being about the hardest of any for a young girl.

I was very pleased that none of my siblings got the scarlet fever.

It would be in the November when we had a letter from Mrs. Bilton (Helen's Mum) asking if I would go and work for her. There was not a lot to do, she said, just to help with the washing up and peeling potatoes, etc.

I was not asked by Mum if I wanted to go, but was told I had to, although it was about twenty-five miles away. She did not know when she would see me again as it was too far to cycle, even if I had had a cycle. I felt she wanted rid of me.

She thought, I suppose, that it was better for me to go to someone I knew. So, by the end of November, I was packed off with a few old clothes in an old suitcase. The farmer fetched me in his car as there was no other means of getting there.

That was the end of my childhood days. The only time I slept at home after that was the two following Novembers. Believe it or not, I was ill both times. Firstly with mumps and the second year with yellow jaundice.

The last week of November was the only time a farm employee got the chance to have a holiday. There could not have been a worse time of year. I missed the kids when I first left home, and felt sorry for them — especially Lawrence. He had been taken back to the orthopaedic hospital for more treatment to his leg. There was only one visiting day a month, and then we had problems getting there. At least he would get three meals a day.

I often wished they all could sit down to the sort of meals that I had but, meals apart, I was not finding life all that 'rosy.' When Mrs. Bilton wrote and said there was not much to do, she omitted to say I should have to be up at six o'clock each morning and not finish until six p.m. — sometimes later. Also she didn't say (although we should have guessed) that beside the four of us, there were six men coming in for three meals a day. They also slept in (as I have mentioned before).

There being no electrical appliances then, I had to light the fire and get a large kettle boiling for a quarter to seven for the mens' breakfast. If the fire was awkward and would not burn, I was in real trouble.

Although I liked Mrs. Bilton and Helen, if I had had a good home and loving parents, I would not have stayed there.

The only time I got off was Sunday night — then I had to go to Chapel with Helen. I would rather have gone to Church, that was my religion, 'if any.' Well, I had been christened and confirmed in a church. We walked to the chapel in the village, which was two miles away, and the farmer and his wife used to give us a ride back in his car. That was my outing for the week, until the next Sunday night.

We eventually got wise to that old farmer and his wife and, while they stopped behind chatting to their friends, we used to run and hide so they had to go home without us. Thus we were then able to walk home with all the other lads and lassies that went our way. We used to tell Mrs. Bilton some yarn or other about how we missed getting a ride back.

One Friday night there was a social in the village school, and we were allowed to go — with the farmer, of course. He would not normally have gone but it was for Chapel funds and his wife provided some of the supper.

Helen introduced me to two of her friends. By the way, Helen was still at school, and two years younger than me — she was thirteen and I was fifteen. Both of her friends had an older brother at the social. One, called Tom, was interested in Helen, while the other, a handsome nineteen year old, was showing an interest in me. His name was Phillip Groves.

I had not taken much notice of boys up to then, but this one I had a real crush on. He asked me to go to Church on Sundays, where he was in the choir, and he would walk home with me. So, at the risk of getting into trouble with Mrs. Bilton, I did go. Luckily she did not seem to mind.

Things did not go quite according to plan. I did not see much of Phillip as, about that time, his mother was taken ill and remained so for many months. Phillip spent his spare time at home and, if he got to Church, he used to go straight home afterwards. I scarcely saw him for the rest of that year.

His mother passed away during the time that I was at my next job.

Discouraged

Life seemed to be all bed and work for me. I was so disappointed not being able to see Phillip, whilst Helen, who was really too young to be having a boyfriend, could see Tom every Sunday night. Sometimes, she could see him during the week because she used to go to their house in the dinner hour with his sister, Dora. They lived near the school.

There seemed to be nothing but work, cleaning other people's dirt up, for me, and for such small wages. I only had five shillings a week. I did realise that I had a lot to be thankful for after my poverty-stricken childhood, such as plenty of good food and a clean, comfortable bed.

Sixteen and Another Move

I had been with the Biltons two years and was now sixteen years old. Helen had left school, so she had to stay at home and do the work that I had been doing. I felt sorry for her, but knew she would not be expected to do all the same as me. Her mother would get up earlier and do a lot more to help.

They were, however, very helpful in getting me another job. It was in the middle of a village, and only three miles from town. It was a large farmhouse, much 'posher' than the Biltons. There was only the farmer and his wife, as they had no children. I was quite over-awed with it and felt like a fish out of water, wondering if I would do things right for them. It was a lovely house with lovely carpets and furniture, the like of which I had never seen before. The Biltons, although much better than I had been used to, was nothing compared with this. I felt they needed someone smarter than me for a maid, but that is the story of my life — always putting myself down.

Anyway they seemed to take to me, and made sure that I didn't have to work such long hours as I had previously. I was finished every day at one o'clock, and was then free to get washed and changed. Sometimes I could walk to the village shop and to the post office, which in itself was a treat. I never got further than the back yard or the clothes line at the Biltons from one Sunday to the next.

I was allowed out from one o'clock until nine on Saturdays and Sundays. By then the buses had started running around the villages so I was able to go to the pictures on a Saturday night — that was a real treat. I soon got to know a couple of the village girls to go with. On Sunday nights we went to Church, then for a walk afterwards, except in winter. Then I would go to one of their houses until it was time for me to go in.

During my second year there I was allowed out on Wednesday nights as well, also getting an extension of time until nine thirty. I can honestly say that the two years I spent there with the Webbs, were the happiest years of my life *up to then*.

Sadly, all good things come to an end, and at eighteen years old I thought it was time I had more money. Although everything else was satisfactory, the wages were not as I only had eight shillings a week. So that November I asked the boss for a rise and was told that he could not pay me at all. His wife would have to do the work, with just a helper on Fridays. He said he was sorry to lose me, but he would help me to find another job — which he did.

The farmers were having a lean time just before the war, a few of them around that area going bankrupt. Strangely the war seemed to put them back on their feet with the grants and subsidies they received.

I was very upset when I left the Webbs, feeling sure I would never get another job like it, and I was right. My next job was in a village a further three miles away. So now I was six miles from town, which disappointed me, as I still could not afford to buy a bicycle.

I stayed there three years and hated nearly every day of it. It was the hardest three years of my life as regards work. I did more before breakfast than most women did all day. It involved getting up at six a.m., cleaning the kitchen grate and lighting the fire, hoping it would light at the first try — there was never any time to be wasted — laying the table in the kitchen for breakfast and cooking the bacon and eggs, or at least getting them into the big iron frying pan which hung over the fire. I then had to go into the dining room and clean the grate out and lay the fire ready for lighting in the afternoon. Also I had to get plenty of coal into the coal scuttles and logs into a basket, so they didn't have to do it.

Following this I then had to get down on my knees with a stiff hand-brush and dustpan and sweep the carpet, it was like a London fog when I had finished. Next, I had to dust the furniture, and there was a lot of it. Endless ornaments had to be lifted and dusted — woe betide me if I left anything. The mistress would rub her fingers on the furniture if I had been a bit quicker than usual, to see if I had missed any.

On Friday mornings it all had to be polished — none of the spray-on stuff then — it was wax which had to be rubbed on. While I was doing this I had to keep on running into the kitchen to see if the fire and the bacon were all right. By this time the family were downstairs, so the mistress looked after the breakfast.

While they were getting their meal, I had to go into the coal shed and clean all the boots, shoes and leather leggings. In winter it was freezing cold and dark, and I had to manage with a candle as they still had not got electric.

All this time the customers were calling for milk or eggs, so I had to keep leaving off to attend to them. When the milkman had finished separating the milk, I had to take the buckets and parts of the separator into another shed and thoroughly wash and scald them. Next I peeled the potatoes for dinner, and in winter I sometimes had to skin a rabbit or hare. That was a job I hated, especially the hares.

By this time they had finished their breakfast and I could have mine. Needless to say, I was ready for it. Ready for a sit down too, some might think. At least there was always plenty of good food, which I think was what kept me going.

Those Yorkshire farmers' wives certainly knew how to put on a good meal. They had plenty of the right stuff to cook with, killing two large pigs each winter, which provided them with plenty of ham and bacon for most of the year. It was cured in salt then hung in the cellar. There was, of course, buckets of lard. From the cows they had milk, cream and butter. The poultry provided plenty of eggs.

Then of course, they had large gardens and orchards.

Every winter they had three or four big shooting days, inviting other farmers. They would then share out their spoils of rabbits, hares, pheasants, partridges and pigeons. What a day it used to be for us as we prepared a big hot meal for when they returned in the late afternoon. The dining table was laden with tempting dishes. It made a lot of work for us, and it was nearly bedtime when all was cleared away.

It always seemed so unfair to me that they had so very much, and the workers so little. After all, where would the boss be without the workers?

Monday, after breakfast, was washing day. This meant carrying buckets of water to fill the copper, under which we used to lay the fire the night before.

30

First of all, we had to sort the clothes — the whites from the coloureds. They then had to be 'dollied' in a zinc tub, wrung through the old mangle, scrubbed in a wooden tub, and the whites wrung out of there and put in the copper to boil. When they came out of the copper they had to be rinsed twice and wrung out again. Certain things then had to be starched before being hung on the line in the garden. What an awful cold job that was in the winter time. Sometimes, when it was freezing, the clothes would be as stiff as boards by the time we got them pegged on the line. My hands used to get chapped and bleeding.

The afternoon was taken up with ironing, using those awful old flat irons, heated in front of the fire.

Tuesday and Friday we had a warmer job — it was baking day.

27

Phillip Finds Me Again

One Saturday afternoon, during my first month at that place, I was cycling to town on a borrowed cycle (the mistress had lent it to me — she never used it now that they had got a car) and I met up with Phillip again. He caught me up on the road, saying he had been told I was working in the village, and he hoped he would see me.

He said he had not been far since his mother's death. He was very upset about it. She had brought up a large family but, as the last child left school, and she could have had an easier time, she fell ill.

However, after spending the afternoon in town, we went to the pictures that night. He told me he worked only two miles to the other side of the village.

I was so pleased to be in touch with him again, as I didn't know anyone in the village, and was not very happy working at the Jones'. Yet I dare not leave in case I could not get another job.

There was no way I would go home to live. In any case, they could not afford to keep me.

My life was made more tolerable knowing Phillip was near and seemed interested in me. I felt we were made for each other, as we had the same interests. We both came from poor families so we knew what poverty was, but his mother had apparently been a better manager than mine. His father had been in the same job all his married life, not always flitting about from one job to another. Once they had got a home together they had kept it.

I dreaded Phillip getting to know my family history, being sure that would be the end of our relationship. Although he often spoke of his own family, he never asked questions about mine.

We did not have a very good courtship. Right out in the country, as we were, there was not much to do. Also, of course, I didn't have much liberty, only being allowed out at the weekend and Wednesday night from 6.30 to 9.30.

Every Saturday night we went to the pictures, (regardless of what was on). I loved it when the lights went out and Phillip put his arm around me. We were transported into another world for a couple of hours — mostly a world of wealth, beauty and glamour. I used to envy those beautiful film stars, and wished I were one of them.

Being so young and gullible, I thought it was all true, but the ride back home in the winter time soon brought me down to earth. Those country roads were cold and dark, the only lights being the ones from our cycle lamps. Sometimes it would be snowing or raining, and no matter how the wind blew, I had to be in the house by 9.30. Mrs. Jones would be waiting in the kitchen looking at the clock and, if I was five minutes late, she wanted an explanation. I used to wish she would try riding a cycle in the wind.

At other times we would go to Phillip's sister for the afternoon and evening. She and I got on very well, which pleased Phillip. Her name was Lynette. He also had a brother who lived quite near to where I worked, so we often went there, especially in the winter.

We never seemed to have much time to ourselves. A kiss and a cuddle at the door, when we said goodnight, was the nearest we got to making love. Perhaps it was just as well we didn't. Mum had found out, somehow or other, that I had a boyfriend (although they lived about fifteen about miles from me) and she had threatened me, if I got pregnant, I would have to go to the workhouse. I hated her for saying that and thought 'What a Mother!'.

Maybe I should have taken some of the blame for her attitude, after all, I scarcely owned them, being away from home from the age of fourteen.

There not being much transport, It was a long way to cycle on that old 'boneshaker' of Mrs. Jones. Also it was very embarrassing having to keep asking to borrow it. She could have given me the old thing, as she had not ridden it for many years. There was no need as they had a nice car.

However, by the third summer that I was there, I had saved up to buy myself a second-hand one. I was as thrilled with that cycle as any young woman of today is with her first car.

28

We Get Engaged

It was the August Bank Holiday of my third year with the Jones' when Phillip and I decided to go to Scarborough for the day. I asked Mrs. Jones for an extension of time out at night, and she was agreeable to letting me stop out until 10 o'clock. She also kindly made us some sandwiches, and filled a flask with tea.

Away we went, setting off about 7.30 in the morning. She laughed at us going so early, but we had to cycle the six miles into town to catch the bus. Then it was a forty-mile ride to Scarborough, with all the stops that a bus has. It was not that early when we got there.

We had a really enjoyable day, with good weather. We were so happy and madly in love by then, and wished we could spend more time together.

In the morning, we walked from one end of Scarborough to the other. Going up Castle Hill at mid-day, we had our sandwiches sitting on the grass and looked down over the town. Phillip said it would be good if we could spend a weekend there the next year.

I was quite excited at the thought of it. I would have loved nothing better than to stay in one of those large hotels, but I knew they were too grand for the likes of us. Only the rich people had that pleasure in those days. We would have to make do with a bed and breakfast place. Even that would be a treat for us.

All this time I was wondering what was going on in Phillip's mind. Did he expect me to sleep with him for the weekend. 'It would be very exciting,' I thought. Mrs. Jones would go berserk if she found out, as she was sure to do in time. She would send me 'packing' in disgrace. Such behaviour was not acceptable in those days.

Up to that point, Phillip had not mentioned marriage or even an engagement. This was probably because I had once said to him that my parents would not let me marry under twenty-one. Now, I had only three weeks to

33

wait for my twenty-first birthday. Then I could do as I liked, but it was not the *done thing* for the girl to ask the boy to marry her.

However, all my questions were answered that night. We must have caught an early bus back and, having got our cycles from the place where we had left them in the morning, were well on our way back to the Jones'. At the top of the hill, which we always had to walk up, Phillip looked at his watch and said it was only a quarter to nine, and only a mile or so left to ride.

We put up our cycles behind some bushes at the road side where no passers-by could see them. Then we sat down on Phillip's mac and ate the few sandwiches which we had left, and then laid back and gazed at the stars that were just beginning to shine.

It reminded me of that dreadful night years before when I, my parents and siblings had to sleep out all night. 'Why did it worry me so?' I thought. After all many people have slept out all night and thought nothing of it.

To get back to my story. Phillip leaned over me and kissed me as never before. Soon his hand was in my button-through dress and the passion was rising in both of us. Needless to say, the inevitable happened. He said he loved me so much, and would I marry him, soon.

I did not hesitate to answer yes, having loved him ever since that first night that I met him nearly six years ago.

On the following Saturday we cycled to town and Phillip bought me an engagement ring. I had never been so happy in all my life, feeling sure I was the only girl in the world to feel so happy. At last, my life had changed for the better.

We arranged to get married on the last Saturday of November. It would not come quick enough for either of us. I suppose we both knew full well what happened that night, would happen again.

I did not want to be pregnant when I married. I wanted a white wedding, in church, with all the trimmings. We should have had to go to the Register Office if I had got pregnant.

After all, I had saved hard out of my small wages for a decent wedding, and to buy all the things that I was supposed to buy for the home. I did not want any children for the first year of our marriage, feeling I deserved a good rest from work first.

It was a few weeks later before I told Mrs. Jones that I was getting married. She was not very well at the time and she sat down and cried, saying she did not know what she would do without me.

It was coming to the time when girls did not want domestic work, now that the buses were running around the villages. They preferred to have jobs in shops and factories where they could get higher wages. They did not take into account that domestic workers got bed and board as part of their wages, with much better food than their parents could give them. Plus, we got good training in house keeping, which is essential to any girl getting married.

Mrs. Jones asked me if I could help her find a girl to take my place. That was easy. I knew just the person, Frances. She wanted to be away from home and was well trained in farmhouse work, having lived in one all her life.

She was twenty-one, and trying to save to get married, so I wrote to her and told her all about it. She cycled to the Jones' the following week, and it was arranged that she take over where I left off.

29

The Wedding

November thirtieth came round at last. Mrs. Jones had made me a three-tier wedding cake, and a friend who lived near, iced it for me free of charge. Several people who came to the Jones' to buy milk, eggs and butter, brought me presents of tablecloths, towels and jugs. I thought how lucky I was.

The wedding day was cold and grey, but it did not dampen our spirits. We had waited impatiently for this day. I had a long white wedding dress, but thought a long veil was too grand for me, so I made do with a white hat.

Mrs. Jones gave me one of her cast-off coats and a hat for my Mum to wear. I had said previously that I wondered what she would turn up in, knowing she had not the money to buy a new outfit. Phillip and I took it the week before the wedding. Luckily, it fitted her well, both women being tall and thin. I don't know what Phillip thought about it, but he did not say anything.

We did not stay long. As usual, everything looked a mess in the house and, as usual, there was an argument going on. I can't remember a time when there wasn't — I think they liked the sound of their voices. I suppose living in such poverty, year after year, with not a hope of things getting any better, especially while the family were young, there was always something to argue about. I used to wish they would part — which they did some years later.

Phillip's home was so neat and orderly. His eldest sister had left her job as a nanny when their mother died to house-keep for her father. I felt sorry for her, as she had got used to a better way of living. Being with titled people and travelling about the country (if, or when, they wanted to take the children with them), she had had a lady's life.

However, I could not risk any upsets on my wedding day, so I refused to be married from home and got married from the Jones' in the village church there. We had the village hall for our reception. Although it was such a dull, cold day, a lot of the village people turned out to see us.

We did not have a honeymoon but went straight to our home which, I forgot to say, was in the village where I had spent two years with the Webbs. It was a lovely four-bedroomed house. I was 'over the moon' when the farmer said we could have it at a rent of five shillings a week. I loved that little village, it was so handy for the town. We could always walk if there was no other means at the time we wanted to go. Luckily, we both had a cycle, so there was no problem.

We bought some lovely old furniture from the sale-room. Mrs. Jones advised us not to buy the new stuff. She said it did not look half as nice as the old — and I think she was right.

She had bought a new bedroom carpet, and gave me the old one. Not many people had wall-to-wall carpet then, so I felt we were lucky to have it. Working people had to make do with lino and clipped rugs, which they made themselves out of old clothes. Mrs. Jones also bought me a lovely pair of wool blankets. She really excelled herself — I had to take back all I had criticised her for.

At last, I was my own mistress and it was wonderful. Life had been so good for me. We were both so happy and so madly in love.

I had made up my mind to be a better housekeeper than my Mother, after all, I had had seven years training, and felt quite capable of doing the task ahead of me.

Furthermore, I was never going to argue with Phillip. Also I did not want a family — one would do for me. In fact, I was going to 'work miracles.'

I forgot to tell myself that I had got off to a better start than my Mother, and that we are not the master of our own fate. However, *she* did not have such a bad life once the children had grown up. She lived to be eighty-two, and Father lived to be ninety-three. They had been parted for many years then.

Phillip gave me his wage packet every Friday night, and on Saturday we would go to town on the bus to do the shopping for groceries, etc. Every week I put some money in the bank, and by the spring we had put nearly all the money back that we had spent on the wedding and the home. I had thirty pounds left and Phillip had nearly four hundred pounds — not bad for the small wages we got. We certainly never wasted money. Phillip had never smoked or drank.

That winter was long and cold and I had some lonely days on my own. I had never been on my own before. Phillip had three miles to cycle to work, so he could not get home at mid-day. We were so pleased to see each other when he came home at six o'clock. He would put his arms around me and kiss me as though he had not seen me for months.

I loved it. He was so big and strong and I felt so well protected. He was not only a husband, but a lover, and a father figure. We truly loved each other and vowed to do so until we were old and grey.

30

Spring Again

In the spring I cycled the three miles to Mrs. Jones' to help with the cleaning. It was a big house and took a lot of doing.

It was nice to be with Frances again, and I had lots to tell her about my new life. She was getting excited at the thought of her marriage the next year.

The light nights had come and Phillip got busy in the garden, digging and planting potatoes and vegetables. I had a plot at the top of the garden where I planted a few flowers. Neither of us knew much about gardening, but we were learning fast.

We had a few visitors in the early part of the summer, the first being Lynette and her husband, Carl. They stayed for the weekend and we had a lovely time together. It was arranged that we would go to their place in a couple of weeks time

Next to come was my aunt and uncle, who just came for a day. They had bought a car, so I suppose they wanted us to see it. Very few working class people had cars then, but they had only had the one child to bring up.

The Worst Shock Of All

It was now the last week of June and the Chapel Anniversary, so we decided to go. It was nice listening to the children saying their pieces of poetry and singing their hymns.

It used to be the big event of the summer in the Yorkshire villages. Lots of the parents would invite their relations and friends from other villages. The Chapel was always full.

Sadly, that is no longer the case. In fact, a lot of Chapels are closed up, or have been sold for other purposes. Television and cars have taken the place of those Chapels and Churches.

On the following Tuesday night they had another service, with a big supper afterwards. We were asked by a few people to go, so we did. What a lovely supper it was, all provided by the local farmers' wives and others. There was ham and salads, cakes, pastries, trifles, the lot — and all for sixpence.

On the way home I said to Phillip that I would write off to another bed and breakfast place in Scarborough, (I had already written to two places and had no answer). It was the first day of July on the morrow.

So, after I had seen Phillip off to work the next day, I set about the housework. That done, I sat down to write.

I had only just started, when there was a knock on the front door. I thought it would be the postman with a letter from one of the guest houses, but no, it was a man in working overalls. I wondered who he was and what he wanted.

He said to me: 'Mrs. Groves, I have been sent to inform you your husband has had an accident. He has been taken to the hospital. You ought to go straight away. I will ask your neighbour to go with you.' My legs turned to jelly. I thought, whatever can have happened to him? I do hope he has not broken any limbs. It will mean him being off work a long time. There will be no Scarborough for us this year. At the same time as I am thinking all that, I am rushing upstairs to change my dress and tidy my hair.

Sally from next door had come rushing in. She was shouting to ask me if she could do anything to help. I asked her to pump my cycle wheel up.

It had a slow puncture, but she said she would go and ask Mr. Webb if he would take us in his car.

They only lived a couple of yards up the street. We could see their house from our front door. Luckily, Mr. Webb was just coming out of his drive as Sally got there, so no time was lost in getting to the hospital.

On arriving there we were kept waiting because the Matron was busy. I wondered why we could not just go into the ward without her help. I was soon to find out why.

When she finally came to us, she turned to Sally and said: 'Are you Mrs. Groves?' To which Sally replied: 'No, this young woman is.' She turned to me in surprise. Sally and I looked more like mother and daughter. She was a tall, big woman of thirty, whereas I was a short five foot, rather thin, twenty-one year old.

The Matron said to me: 'Will you come this way, please.' I thought she was leading us into the men's ward, but no, she turned into what turned out to be her sitting room. She closed the door and, turning to me, she said: 'I am sorry to inform you, your husband is *dead*'.

I was struck dumb. All I could say was: 'dead.' I thought he could not be. He was a strong, healthy, twenty-six year old. How could he be dead? My next thought was, they have got our names mixed with someone else. Groves was a rather common name around that area.

The Matron then turned to me and said: 'If it is of any consolation to you, he did not suffer. Death was instantaneous.'

Sally was crying her eyes out, yet I had not shed a tear. I was so stunned and shocked, and refused to believe it until I had seen him. I asked Matron if I could go and see him, but she insisted I wait until his father came — they had already sent for him. Then, she said, we could go into the mortuary together.

I shall never forget it. It was the first time I had been in such a place and, in fact, the first body I had seen (apart from baby George). Even after seeing Phillip laid there, I still could not believe he was dead. I could not cry at first, I was struck numb, and was as cold as ice. I said to myself: 'Dear God, what have we done to deserve this?' We had been so happy, and now it had all been snatched away. I felt useless without Phillip. He had protected and loved me as I knew no-one else ever had, or ever would. All I wanted now was to die. There seemed nothing left to live for.

At his father's request, he was buried in the village churchyard. The village where he, and his father before him, had been born, and where his mother was buried.

I went to stay with Lynette for a week after the funeral. Then she spent a week with me, to try to settle me in. When she went back, I got a young friend out of the village to come to sleep. I was so nervous on my own, but I wanted to keep the house on and, therefore, my independence.

I had lots of offers from kind friends and relations on Phillip's side to go and live with them, but I knew it would not be long before I outstayed my welcome. After all, they were all young and bringing up their families. It would not have worked out. I must admit, I felt a pang of jealousy seeing them with their husbands, and especially their babies — a pleasure which I should never know now. Or so I thought at that time.

I cycled the six miles every Sunday with flowers for Phillip's grave, until the winter weather made it impossible, and spent my £30 on a grave stone. I thought I had had a miserable childhood, but that was nothing compared with the misery I felt then.

Mrs. Jones gave me some work, and I was glad of it. The widows' pension was only ten shillings a week, five of that going on the rent. I got the *handsome* sum of four hundred pounds for Phillip's death which I could only have at one pound ten shillings per week. It was an insult, but there was nothing I could do about it as I had no-one to help me fight the case. Of course at that time I was too miserable to think straight about money, or my future.

I should have said before that Phillip was working on a large building site when he was killed. He was on the ground floor, when someone higher up dropped a plank on his head, killing him instantly. They were supposed to have had a safety net, but they didn't.

32

More Sad Memories

That first Christmas after Phillip's death, Mrs. Jones invited me to go to their house for dinner. Of course, I was expected to get there in time to help Frances to cook it, while they went to church.

As long as I live I shall remember that ride there. It was a beautiful sunny morning, not much like what we expect in England at Christmas. All the same, it had been a very hard frost the night before.

I stopped on the top of the hill and looked at the spot where Phillip and

I had made love and planned our marriage. The sun glistened on the frosty fields. As I stood there, I could hear three lots of church bells ringing out across the countryside, coming from different directions — including the ones where Phillip lay.

The pain in my heart was unbearable, and I wondered how long I could go on living with it. If only I could have died as well.

'In such a short time how one's life can be changed.' None of us can be sure of the future, perhaps it is as well we cannot know. Frances seemed to be pleased to see me. It must have been awkward for her, not knowing what to say to me when I was so miserable.

The Jones' arrived back from church, all done up in their Sunday best. Mrs. Jones gave me a very pretty teapot for a Christmas present. Frances and I had a little chuckle to ourselves, seeing how big it was when she knew I was on my own. All the same, I had it for many years.

I stayed there until Boxing Day, then cycled back home. Mary, the young woman who came to sleep, asked me to their house for tea. The following week I went on the bus to York, and from there to my Aunt Elsie, for a week. I used to think I could get away from my sorrow, but it was no use, it went with me. Every time I returned home it seemed to start again from day one. I suppose that is how it is for everyone who loses a loved one.

Aunt Elsie was good to me, and tried her best to cheer me up. I could have sold up and gone to live with them. She said she thought of me as the daughter they never had, but I wanted to keep my home and independence.

That winter dragged on, and I hated the long dark nights. We had not got the television then to entertain us, only an old wireless. I don't know why they were called that, they seemed to be *all* wires. I suppose we were lucky to have one. Not many working class people had them at that time. Most did have a wind-up gramophone.

In the spring, Lynette and Carl came for a weekend, and he dug and planted the garden for me. It was nice to see them again. I went to their house later in the year for a week.

41

33

The First Anniversary

July the first came round — the first anniversary of Phillip's death. I began to settle down a bit after that. I was not always looking back to the previous year. No doubt the first year is the worst for everyone after a death. I knew life would never be the same again, but I was only twenty-two years old — I had a long way to go.

Towards the end of July it was the Chapel trip day. I was asked if I would like to go as there were one or two seats left on the bus. Having nothing better to do that day I said yes, I would go.

The trip was to the seaside. I had a look round the shops in the morning, then went for lunch. In the afternoon I got a deck chair and sat on the sands, quite near to a fortune teller's tent. I was amazed at the number of people who went in and out, both men and women.

I thought I would go in and have 'half a crown's worth.' She told me I had a long life ahead of me. I should die aged 91, but I should be on crutches. Also, I should have four children. 'What a laugh', I thought. I should never be rich, but, I should never want for a crust, and that I should travel overseas.

I came out of her tent feeling I had wasted my money. I was not very pleased with myself for doing so, but the future years brought a few surprises.

34

At The Dance

That summer passed by uneventfully, then the dark nights were on us again. It was the middle of November, and there was a dance in the schoolroom in aid of church funds. Mary asked me if I would go with her. I didn't really want to and, furthermore, I was no good at dancing, but said I would go.

I just sat there and watched them all enjoying themselves. The room was packed, a lot of young people from the town had come, as they always did when the dances were for the church. Not because they were all religious, but because of the good supper that was always provided. Everyone in the village contributed something, the tables were laden.

About half-way through the night, a dark wavy-haired young man came to me and asked for a dance, but I had to tell him I couldn't. So he sat with me for the rest of the night, then walked home with Mary and I. He said his name was Simon Willis, and asked me to go to the cinema the next night. I said no, again, as I felt it was too soon to be getting interested in young men.

It was sometime after Christmas before I saw him again. I was shopping in town one Saturday afternoon, when I met him. He asked me again to go to the cinema. So this time I said I would, mainly because I wanted to see that particular film. I had heard it was very good. I remember it was 'Rio Rita.'

That was the first time I had been to the cinema since Phillip's death. Of course, it brought back more sad memories. I felt guilty sitting there with another young man, and could not help thinking what Phillip would think of me if he could have known. Yet all my friends, and even his relations, were telling me to get out more and find myself another partner. I was very young.

Even Lynette said I could not spend the rest of my life alone. Nothing I could do would hurt Phillip now. Yet it was a few weeks before I dared ask Simon to my house. I was sure the neighbours would have a 'field day' gossiping about me. Had I lived in a large town, no-one would have noticed, but in a small village it was a different matter. Everyone seemed to know everyone else's business.

All the same, I will not criticise too much. Those village folk are the 'salt of the earth' when anyone is in trouble. They rally round and help — nothing is too much trouble for them.

So when I did invite Simon for the first time, I also invited his married sister and her husband as well, just to make it look better. Simon was a nice man, two years younger than me. We got on well together.

Two years later, on August fifth, we got married. We just had a quiet wedding. I wore a navy suit and did not have any bridesmaids. It was in the village church, with about thirty guests, and a small reception at home. My uncle gave me away as my parents had moved back to Cambridgeshire. We went to Morecambe for our honeymoon, and had only been back three weeks when the Second World War started. Just as I thought I was going to start life anew.

Three evacuee boys, all thirteen year olds, were dumped on us whether we wanted them or not. They were from the city of Hull, nice boys really, but city life is very different from a small village in the country. They found it hard to settle down. By Christmas they had all gone back.

Simon had got his papers by then to go for his medical, prior to joining the army. I felt that I was not meant to be married, or for that matter, to be happy.

I must admit we were not too worried at that early stage of the war, everyone seemed positive it would not last long. 'Little did we know.' We certainly under-estimated Hitler's power.

However, it was eighteen months before Simon got his call-up papers. Our daughter Elizabeth was born just six weeks before he went. She was going to school when he came back.

The first year, when he was training at Aldershot, he got home on a forty-eight hour leave every twelve weeks. After that, he was sent to Italy and then to Greece. We wrote to each other nearly every day. I tried to keep him up with Elizabeth's progress, and regularly had photos taken of her. We were always hoping and praying for an end to the war so we could be together again.

What a time it was for all of us — always fearing the German bombers coming over at night. We never seemed to get a good night's sleep. Still, I won't elaborate on the war years, I am sure everyone knows all about it. Sufficient to say, Simon arrived home safe and sound, and all in one piece, on my birthday 1946.

So we started life again. We were all so relieved the war was over at last. The saddest part was the loss of those poor young lads who didn't return.

35

Two Years Later

It was now 1948. In May of that year our son Richard was born. I had always said I only wanted one child. I did not want a house full and be poverty stricken, but it was nice for Simon to have a son. He had missed all of Elizabeth's young years.

The next few years were happier for everyone. At last, the shops were filling up again with all the things we had had to do without during the war. Although certain things were still on ration in 1953. It was the year of our Queen's Coronation, and the year we got our first television. What excitement that was!

In May, a week after Richard's fifth birthday, our second daughter was born. We named her Mary Alicia. Then, in July 1954, we had another son, James. So all my plans had gone wrong, but the gypsy's prophecy had come true. Another of her prophecies came true a few years later

I was now forty years old, and I felt much too old to be having babies. Life had become hard for me again with six of us in the house, two of them babies, and no water. The house I had loved so much in the beginning had suddenly become very hard work.

I kept asking Simon to look for a more modern house in town, where he worked. As I pointed out, it would save on bus fares. Several working class people that we knew had taken the plunge, and borrowed money to buy their own house. Simon was always reluctant to, as he put it, 'have a mill stone around his neck.'

However, the time came in December 1960 that the landlord died, and his estate had to be sold. We had no option but to find somewhere else. I had been in it 25 years then. It held both sad and happy memories for me. I was sorry in some ways to leave it.

36

A Good Move

We were lucky enough to find a very nice house in the town, but this time we had to borrow money to buy it. We never regretted it though, as we worked hard and had it paid for in twelve years.

I took pride in redecorating it. Little James was six years old, so I had had a long wait to get a modern house. I had been wanting one since he was born.

Every morning I would get them off to school. They had cooked dinners at school in those days, so I had the full day to myself to get on with the work. I would cycle to town to our new house and do as much wallpapering and painting as I could. Then I would cycle back in time to catch Mary and James coming out of school.

We had arranged to move into the house on 29th March, so on the 21st I stayed at home and proceeded to pack the small items into boxes ready for moving.

Young James came running in from school that afternoon, and asked if he could go and play with his friends. I said: 'Yes, but mind when you cross the road.' But no, he was in too big a hurry. He ran in front of a car which was following a lorry and was knocked down. He let the lorry go by and must not have seen the car coming. Although he did not seem to have much wrong with him, we sent for the doctor, just in case. He said we had to let him rest, which we did, but in the night he died in his sleep. A small blood clot had touched his brain.

The grief and misery we all felt at the time will never be forgotten. We buried him in the village churchyard on the following Monday, and moved to our fresh house on the Wednesday.

All the pleasure we had had looking forward to it had now gone. I tried to keep calm about it, for the sake of Richard and Mary, as I could see it was affecting them badly. Especially Mary. Being so close in ages, they were almost like twins, always playing together.

It took us *all* a long time to get over it, in fact, we still talk about him with a lump in our throats. I often wonder why some of us have such bad luck, while others go through life with no real trauma. I should have said that by this time Elizabeth was married, too young we thought, but she had a good husband and a nice modern house, just the other side of town. They were very happy.

I missed her terribly at first, but we get used to all things in time. At least she was alive and well, and not too far away.

Mary stayed at home with us until she was twenty three, and when she married she also lived near. I could say we have never been parted, except on the *very rare* holidays we have had. She now has two lovely daughters, whom Simon and I adore.

Elizabeth has two fine sons. Sad to say, they have grown up without us scarcely knowing them. When the eldest one was nine years old, she wrote to ask if they could come home for the weekend. I should have said before that it was soon after James' death. They had moved further away, much further, and in a lonely place which was awkward to get to. She said that she had something to tell us.

46

I jumped to conclusions, and said to Simon: 'I bet there's another baby on the way.'

He said it was more likely they were moving. I worried myself sick, thinking they might be moving even further away, where we couldn't get to see them.

What a shock we got when they came. She said they had applied to emigrate to *Australia*. I was stunned. We were still grieving over James, and now she wanted to go right out of our lives. I was sure it would be for ever, if they did go. We hadn't much money — no hopes of getting four of us there to see them. I knew it would take them a long time to get a house and a home together.

It was easy for them to get to Australia in those days — they could go for £10 each. It was a different matter getting back if they did not settle down.

Well, they got permission to go, passed medicals, etc., and left on January 1st 1969. They spent their last week with us after they had got rid of their home. I shall never forget that cold January morning. There was a light covering of snow the night before. We all went to the station with them, to see them off on the train, then walked home in tears. I felt we had been to a mass funeral and buried them all. I was so positive we should never see any of them again, but nothing is certain in this life, is it?

We did see them again, although it took six long years to do so. It was the occasion of Mary's wedding. They had saved up enough, and the four of them came. That was an exciting time for all of us, looking forward to the wedding, and to them coming. They stayed six weeks, three weeks before the wedding, and three weeks after.

What excitement there was the day Elizabeth, and all of them, arrived. We all, along with her in-laws, went to the station to meet them off the train. The boys had grown so much, and even Elizabeth seemed to have altered.

The wedding was a grand affair, held in the church, with the reception in a beautiful old mansion house. Luckily it was a fine, sunny day. We invited all the relations and friends, so Elizabeth could see them all without travelling about too much.

The six weeks flew past and, of course, their departure was painful again, when they returned to Australia. We didn't know when, or if, we should see them again. I promised I would do my best to save and go there and, true to my word, I did go.

I let Mary's room to a young woman, and got more domestic work. Although the pay wasn't much, I managed to get my fare together by November the following year.

I flew out on a Qantas plane, and admit I was more than a little nervous about flying. I had never been on a plane before in my life — never even seen such an enormous plane — and the prospect of going on my own did not help.

True enough, I was not on my own on the plane, but I did not know any other passengers. However, I was put on the side, with two other elderly ladies, one of whom never shut up about her marvellous grandchildren.

Elizabeth met me at the airport. It was so exciting seeing her again, coupled with that feeling of having flown across the world and landing in another country.

I spent six happy weeks with Elizabeth and her husband and family. They all put themselves out to make my holiday a good one. I was very upset when I left, wondering if that would be our last meeting.

I need not have worried, as I did see them again three years later, when I accompanied a neighbour of ours. She wanted to go to Australia to see a relation of hers, but was nervous of going alone. Her name was Elsie, and her relation lived not far from Elizabeth. We were able to meet up during the holiday a few times, and we became very good friends after that.

Two years later Simon retired from work, he was sixty five by then, and we both went to Australia for three months. Simon had not seen Elizabeth for six years, so he was really looking forward to going. That is where another of the fortune-teller's prophecies came true — going overseas.

Richard had married in 1971, and we thought they were happy. Evidently, his wife was not. Although they were together for thirteen years, she finally went off with another young man. We were very upset for Richard. Luckily they didn't have a family, so there was no tug-of-war there. I am pleased to say he met a young lady sometime later, and they are happily married.

37

Another Shock

Life seems to be full of shocks for some people.

It was January of 1986 when Mary's husband, Ian, walked into our house and announced that they had applied to emigrate to Australia, and asked us if we would go as well.

Simon immediately said yes, although a few days later he had second thoughts. However, there was no need at that stage to get too serious about it, after all, they might not get permission to go.

We talked about it many times during the next few weeks. Neither of us could bear the thought of not seeing their two girls grow up. They were only two years and six years old then. I had played such a big part in their lives — looking after them so Mary could go back to work. This especially applied to Katie, the older one. Emily, the younger one, I did not have quite so much as Mary only worked part-time then. I loved both of them as much as if they were my own.

However, by the middle of the year, they had got permission to emigrate, had their medicals, got their passports and everything. All they had to do then was to start packing boxes full of stuff to be sent by sea and, of course, put their house up for sale.

So, seeing it was definite they were going, we set about applying for permission to go. It took a few months, but we did get it. We should have been very upset if we had been turned down.

Mary, Ian and family left England on the day after Boxing Day, 1986. As soon as they had gone we put our house up for sale, and started packing boxes to go by sea. It was upsetting parting with the home we had had for so long, and the house we had had for twenty six years, although I have to admit it was too big for us. We should have had to sell it eventually.

It took until the middle of June to sell it. Then we had to send the furniture, some of which Phillip had bought all those years ago, to the sale room. A lot of our treasures were given away.

We tearfully left old England on 27th July. I suppose the biggest upset was leaving Richard behind. He said he would apply to emigrate when we got settled down — so that made us feel a bit better. As it was, soon after we left, he met the young lady who is now his wife. They both have good jobs, so I can't expect them to come here.

It is nice that we can keep in touch by telephone, and they have both been here for a holiday. I was pleased they were able to come and see how, and where, we live.

We settled down well, and never regretted coming here. We have made some nice friends, and love Australia. Especially the sun and blue skies in summer.

38

No Happy Ending

Well, dear readers, I cannot give you a happy ending to my story. I am in the depths of misery once again

On March 22nd, the anniversary of little James' death, my husband, Simon, was in the garden when, without warning, he dropped dead. I am trying to come to terms with it, telling myself we have had our three score years and ten. He was 75 and I am 78 years old. It is hard, having been retired for ten years, and hardly ever out of each other's sight for twenty four hours a day. I can't help but miss him terribly. I look at his empty chair, and wonder why.

If the fortune-teller is going to be right again, I have a lot of lonely years ahead of me.

Thank heaven for my two daughters here, and my son in England, who I can speak to on the telephone.

Perhaps next year, I shall go to England again for a holiday, and renew old acquaintances. We have kept in touch with them all, by letter and phone.

39

In Conclusion

One long, lonely year has passed since Simon's death. I have just about come to terms with his loss, with a lot of help from my family and friends. Writing this book has passed away a few lonely hours — also trying to keep our rather large garden tidy. I love doing it, but I have not got the energy I used to have for work.

In October, my dear friend Frances, and a friend of hers, paid me a visit. I could not believe it when she wrote and said she was coming, I was so pleased.

We went on two good tours. Firstly, to Alice Springs and Ayers Rock on the 'Ghan' train. That was quite an experience for all of us. We left Melbourne at night and travelled on the 'Overlander' train to Adelaide.

Having four hours to wait there, before boarding the 'Ghan', we went on a tour of Adelaide by means of a small bus, which was waiting just outside the station. We saw much more of the city than I had had seen on a previous visit there. It is a lovely city, and well worth a visit.

We all enjoyed Alice Springs, travelling extensively around that area, including a trip to Ayers Rock to see the Aborigines in the Bush. We learned a lot about their way of life — a life that none of us would envy.

Arriving back from there, we next went to Sydney on a coach, and I think we did not miss anything there. We had a good driver, who took us to all the places of interest.

Back at Melbourne, we went around all the places of interest there, with the help of my daughters, as I cannot drive a car.

All too soon, their holiday was over, and they returned to England. No doubt, they were tired out and ready for a good rest. I'm sure they enjoyed their visit 'Down Under.'

Christmas came round again, but we did not feel like celebrating without Simon. We had a very quiet time.

By the middle of January, I had made up my mind to visit England for what, no doubt, will be the last time. After all, I am getting too old to travel alone. I shall be eighty years old next birthday.

So, at the beginning of March, I flew out of Tullamarine Airport and landed here, to face the cold English winter. A few times I wished I had waited a few weeks longer, until it was a bit warmer, but, no grumbling now. It is nearly time to return.

I have enjoyed my time here visiting old friends and relations. Sadly, one or two have passed away, including my eldest brother, Jamie. His widow is like the rest of us widows — she is having to cope with life on her own. She does have a lot of help from her family, the same as I do. Sister Annie is in a nursing home. She has a few complaints. Douglas, poor lad, is dying of bone cancer. He knows he can't live much longer, but he is very brave, and quite prepared for death. I admire him for his fortitude.

The brother who was crippled with polio, all those years ago, died about ten years ago.

Two younger brothers I cannot trace. I suppose they are all right. 'No news is good news,' as the saying goes.

Now, I am looking forward to seeing my family in Australia and, after a visit to Cornwall, I shall be returning there.

I wish my story could have been a happier one, but God has a plan for us all. We must not grumble.

I WAS SORRY FOR MYSELF
WHEN I HAD NO SHOES.
UNTIL I MET A MAN
WHO HAD NO FEET.